W9-CPE-609

Oliver   Besman
Great Neck, NY, U.S.A.

BASIC / NOT BORING

SCIENCE

Grades 2-3

Inventive Exercises to Sharpen Skills and Raise Achievement

Series Concept & Development
by Imogene Forte & Marjorie Frank
Exercises by Marjorie Frank

Incentive Publications, Inc.
Nashville, Tennessee

About the cover:
    Bound resist, or tie dye, is the most ancient known method of
    fabric surface design. The brilliance of the basic tie dye design
    on this cover reflects the possibilities that emerge from the
    mastery of basic skills.

Illustrated by Kathleen Bullock
Cover art by Mary Patricia Deprez, dba Tye Dye Mary®
Cover design by Marta Drayton, Joe Shibley, and W. Paul Nance
Edited by Anna Quinn

ISBN 978-0-86530-398-0

4   5   6   7   8   9   10   07

PRINTED IN THE UNITED STATES OF AMERICA
www.incentivepublications.com

TABLE OF CONTENTS

Introduction: Celebrate Basic Science Skills 7

Skills Checklist 8

Skills Exercises 9

Is It Alive? . . . (Life Characteristics) 10

Something's Missing . . . (Plant Parts) 11

Circles Everywhere . . . (Life Cycle of Seed Plants) 12

Photo-What? . . . (Photosynthesis) 13

What Do Bees Know? . . . (Flower Parts) 14

Animals With & Without . . . (Animal Classification) 15

Creeping Creatures . . . (Animal Classification) 16

Wormy Questions . . . (Animal Characteristics) 17

Vertebrates on Wheels . . . (Vertebrate Classification) 18

Mix-up at the Zoo . . . (Vertebrate Classification) 20

How Those Animals Behave! . . . (Animal Behavior) 21

Home, Sweet Home . . . (Animal Homes) 22

Who's Who in the Community? . . . (Communities) 23

Looking for Habitats . . . (Habitats) 24

Eco-Puzzle . . . (Ecology) 26

Earth Care . . . (Pollution & Conservation) 27

Too Much Pollution . . . (Pollution) 28

Plenty of Bones . . . (Skeletal System) 29

Body Parts in Hiding . . . (Body Systems) 30

Body Talk . . . (Vocabulary) 31

Aches & Pains . . . (Diseases & Injuries) 32

Health Opposites . . . (Health Behaviors) 33

Refrigerator Inspection . . . (Nutrition) 34

Unsafe! . . . (Safety) 35

Bodies in Space . . . (Solar System) 36

Space Maze . . . (Solar System) 37

Surface Search . . . (Earth Surface Features) 38

Cracks & Rumbles . . . (Earthquakes & Volcanoes) 40

Slow? Or Sudden? . . . (Earth Changes) 41

Underwater Treasure Hunt . . . (The Ocean) 42

Deep-Sea Facts . . . (Waves • Ocean Bottom) 43

What's the Matter? . . . (States of Matter) 44

A Matter of Change . . . (Changes in Matter) 45

The Air up There . . . (Air • Atmosphere) 46

Ready for Anything . . . (Weather) 47

Lost in the Clouds . . . (Clouds & Weather) 48

Pushing & Pulling . . . (Force) 50

Hidden Machines . . . (Simple Machines) 51

The Sound of the Drum . . . (Sound) 52

Hot Words . . . (Heat) 53

Where Would You Find It? . . . (Science Vocabulary) 54

Appendix

Science Words to Know 55

Science Skills Test 58

Answer Key 62

CELEBRATE BASIC SCIENCE SKILLS

Basic does not mean boring! There is certainly nothing dull about . . .

   . . . tracking down mysterious forces and hidden machines
   . . . finding out what bees know that you don't
   . . . coming face to face with a worm
   . . . looking for backbones in alligators and scorpions
   . . . finding your way through mazes to hidden planets or sunken treasure
   . . . separating out the spiders from the other bugs on the wall
   . . . getting to know your way around a skeleton
   . . . investigating clouds, earthquakes, and your refrigerator

The world of science is full of fascination for young students. This book will capture some of that natural interest and use it to sharpen skills.

Each page invites young learners to try a high-interest, visually attractive exercise that will sharpen one specific content skill.

The book can be used in many ways:

- to review or practice a science skill with one student
- to sharpen the skill with a small or large group
- to stimulate a lesson that an adult will present to one or more students
- to assess how well a student has grasped a specific skill

Each page has simple directions. It is intended that an adult be available to help students read the information on the page, if help is needed. In most cases, the pages will best be used as a follow-up to a lesson or concept which has been taught. These are also excellent tools for immediately reinforcing or assessing a student's understanding of the concept.

In order for students to get the best use of the pages, resources and references such as a science text, a set of encyclopedias, and other science information, will be helpful to the students and adults who are working with these pages.

As your students take on the challenges of these enticing adventures with science, they will grow! And as you watch them check off the basic science skills they've acquired or strengthened, you can celebrate with them.

The Skills Test

Use the skills test beginning on page 58 as a pretest and/or post-test. This will help you check the students' mastery of basic science skills and prepare them for success on achievement tests.

SKILLS CHECKLIST
SCIENCE, GRADES 2-3

✔	SKILL	PAGE(S)
	Describe characteristics and needs of living things	10
	Identify parts of some plants	11–14
	Identify some characteristics and processes of plants	12, 13
	Examine the life cycle of seed plants	12
	Identify parts of flowers and their functions	14
	Classify some animal groups	15, 16, 18-20
	Identify characteristics of some animal groups	15–20
	Describe some animal behaviors	21
	Match animals with their homes and habitats	22, 24, 25
	Describe ways organisms interact in their communities	23
	Identify and define some ecology concepts	26
	Identify some kinds of pollution and conservation	27, 28
	Describe characteristics of different body systems	29, 30
	Define and use vocabulary related to the human body	31
	Define some diseases and ailments of the human body	32
	Identify and describe some ways to take care of your health	33, 34
	Identify some safety behaviors and skills	35
	Describe the relationship of bodies in the solar system	36, 37
	Identify and compare objects in space	36, 37
	Identify some landforms on the Earth's surface	38, 39
	Identify some changes to the Earth's surface	40
	Describe Earth changes caused by internal processes	41
	Identify some features of the ocean and the ocean bottom	42, 43
	Identify properties and states of matter	44, 45
	Describe and define some changes in matter	45
	Identify some properties of air and the Earth's atmosphere	46, 48, 49
	Recognize some types of clouds	48, 49
	Describe different kinds of precipitation and weather conditions	47
	Recognize the results of force; identify some forces	50
	Identify some simple machines	51
	Identify some characteristics and properties of sound	52
	Identify some characteristics and properties of heat	53
	Define and use science vocabulary terms	54

SCIENCE
Grades 2-3

Skills Exercises

Is It Alive?

Here are 7 things that are true of living things.

Am I alive? How can you tell?

1. They use food.
2. They grow.
3. They breathe air or take in air.
4. They move.
5. They respond to things around them.
6. They give off wastes.
7. They make other living things like themselves.

Follow the directions below each picture. Then color the picture.

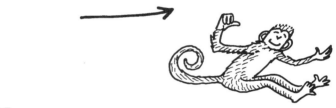

4. _____

1. _____

5. _____

2. _____

6. _____

3. _____

7. _____

Name _____

Something's Missing

Abby is confused about these plants. They seem to be missing some parts. What's missing? Name the plant parts that are described below. Then decide which parts are missing from these plants, and draw them where they belong.

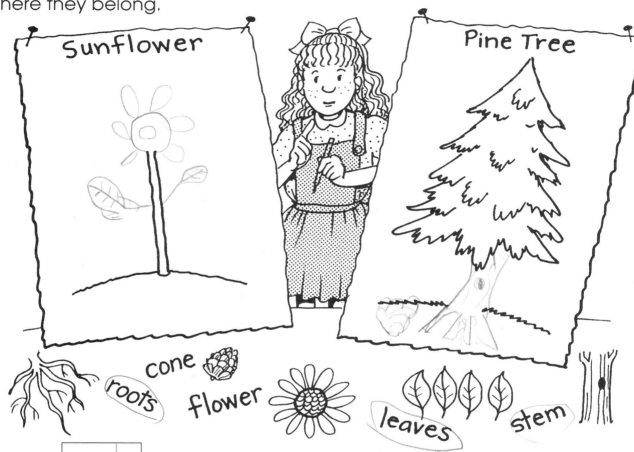

1. The ⬚roots⬚ hold the plant in the ground. They take in water and nutrients from the soil.

2. The ⬚stem⬚ holds up the leaves. It carries water and nutrients to the plant.

3. The ⬚leaves⬚ use air, water, and sunlight to make food for the plant.

4. The ⬚flower⬚ is the place where fruits and seeds form.

5. The ⬚cone⬚ is where seeds form in plants like pine or fir trees.

Name ____Oliver_____

Plant Parts

Circles Everywhere

Lots of things in life go around in circles. One of the most important circles is a life cycle. The life of a plant goes in a circle. A seed lives and grows. It becomes a plant. The plant makes more seeds. The seeds it makes give life to new plants.

Draw the pictures that show the life cycle of a pine tree.

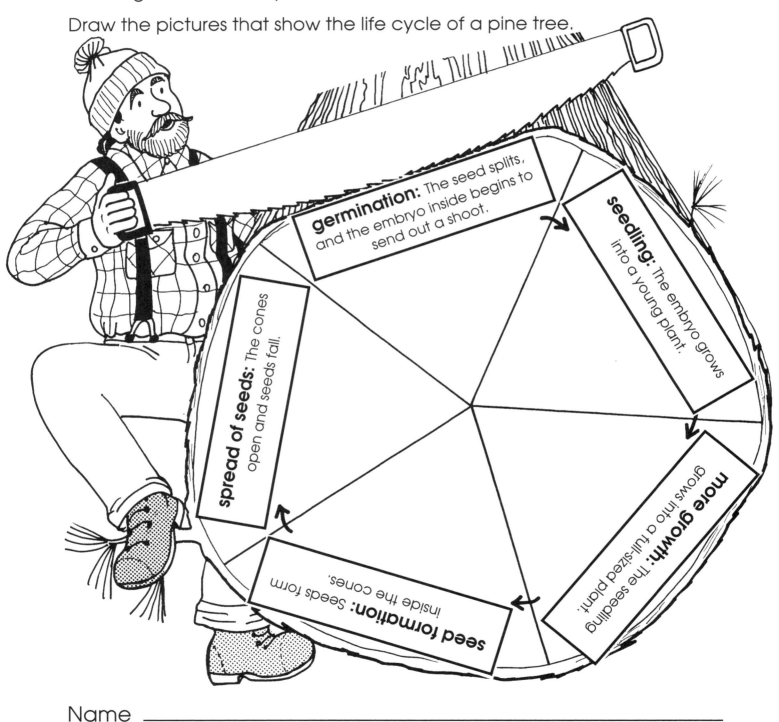

germination: The seed splits, and the embryo inside begins to send out a shoot.

seedling: The embryo grows into a young plant.

spread of seeds: The cones open and seeds fall.

more growth: The seedling grows into a full-sized plant.

seed formation: Seeds form inside the cones.

Name _____

Life Cycle of Seed Plants

Basic Skills/Science 2-3

Photo-What?

Photosynthesis is a huge word about plants. Does it mean that plants know how to take photos? Not really!

Finish this puzzle with the words below to show that you know some things about how photosynthesis works.

Photosynthesis is the process in which plants use air, water, nutrients, and sunlight to make food.

Across

1. _____ dioxide is a part of air used by the plant to make food.
2. Plants need this to make chlorophyll and to make food.
3. These tiny openings in leaves allow them to get air.
4. This gas is given off by the plant during photosynthesis.
5. Plants take air in through their _____.

Down

1. This makes the plant green and helps it make food.

stomata   sunlight   oxygen   carbon   chlorophyll   leaves

Name _____

What Do Bees Know?

Bees spend a lot of time around flowers. They know which part of a flower will supply food for them. Read about the flower parts. Then decide which bee is visiting each part. Write the letter of that bee on the line.

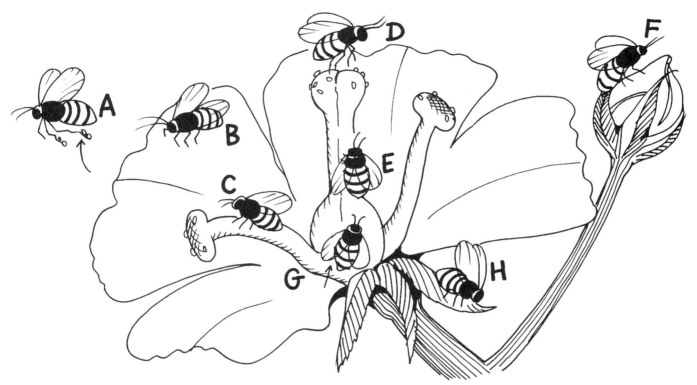

___B___ 1. The **petals** protect the inside parts of the flower. They attract bees who bring pollen from other flowers.

_____ 2. A **bud** is a young flower that is not open yet.

_____ 3. The **sepals** cover and protect the flower bud before it opens.

_____ 4. The **pistil** in the center contains the ovary where seeds are made.

_____ 5. The **stigma** is the sticky top of the pistil. Pollen grains stick to it and send down tubes into the ovary to make seeds.

_____ 6. The **stamens** produce pollen.

_____ 7. The **ovary** is where seeds grow.

_____ 8. **Pollen grains** contain cells that join with egg cells in the ovary and produce new seeds.

Name _____

Animals With & Without

Nicholas has a pretty amazing collection of animals in his backyard. These animals can all be divided into two large groups: animals with backbones and animals without backbones.

Color all the vertebrates in the picture.

Animals with backbones are called **vertebrates**.

Animals **without** backbones are called **invertebrates**.

Name _____

Creeping Creatures

When Lucy opened her eyes this morning, she was shocked and surprised! A whole collection of creatures had gathered on her wall.

Some of them were **insects**. Insects have 3 body sections, 6 legs, and 2 antennae. Draw a red circle around all the insects.

Some of them were **arachnids** (spiders). Arachnids have 8 legs and no antennae. Draw a blue box around all the arachnids.

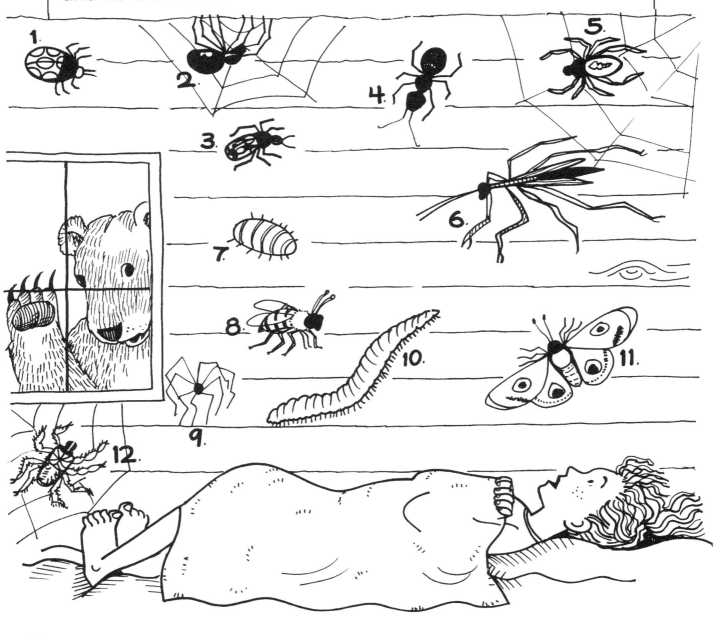

Name _____

Animal Classification

Basic Skills/Science 2-3

Wormy Questions

There are millions of earthworms all over the world. But how much do you know about them? Does an earthworm have legs? Can you tell its head from its tail? How does it move?

Use the words down the side to finish these wormy statements. If you need some help, use your science book.

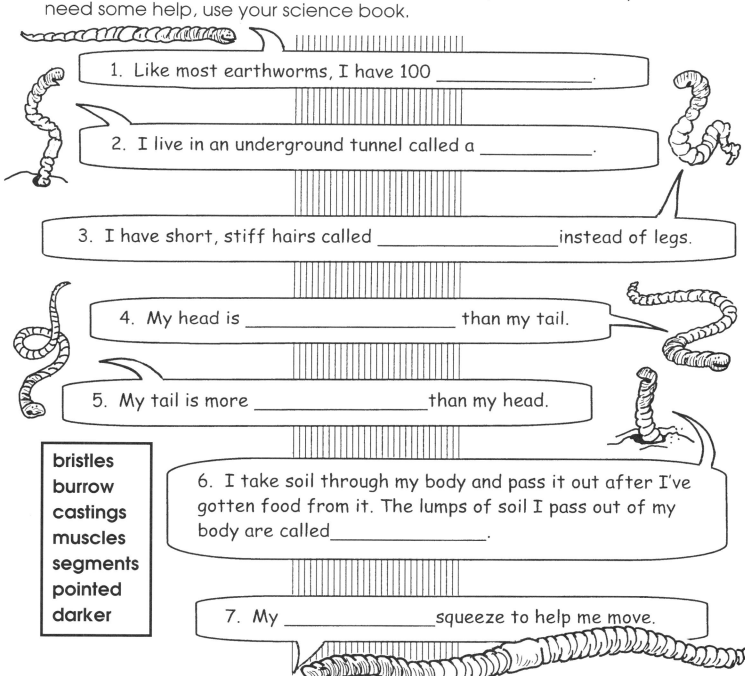

1. Like most earthworms, I have 100 _____.

2. I live in an underground tunnel called a _____.

3. I have short, stiff hairs called _____ instead of legs.

4. My head is _____ than my tail.

5. My tail is more _____ than my head.

bristles
burrow
castings
muscles
segments
pointed
darker

6. I take soil through my body and pass it out after I've gotten food from it. The lumps of soil I pass out of my body are called_____.

7. My _____ squeeze to help me move.

Name _____

Vertebrates on Wheels

Do you remember that vertebrates are animals with backbones?
There are 5 different groups of vertebrates.

On these 2 pages, there is a wheel for each group. Some words or
pictures are missing from the wheels. Look at
the list. Write each word or draw each
picture on the right wheel.

give milk to young
breathe only with gills
feathers
wings
fins
live on land or water
cold-blooded
smooth, moist skin
most fly
hair or fur
warm-blooded
scales
cold-blooded
babies grow inside mother
scaly, dry skin

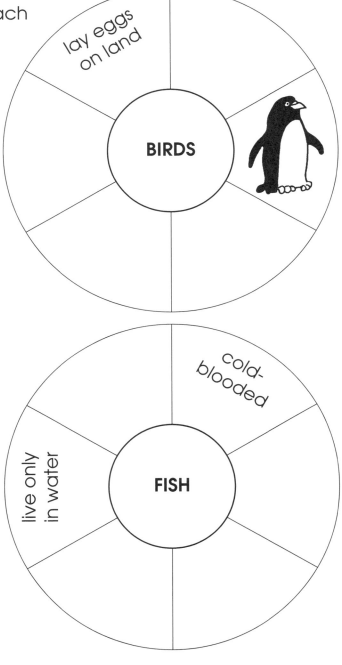

Name _____

Use with page 19.

Vertebrate Classification

Vertebrates on Wheels, continued . . .

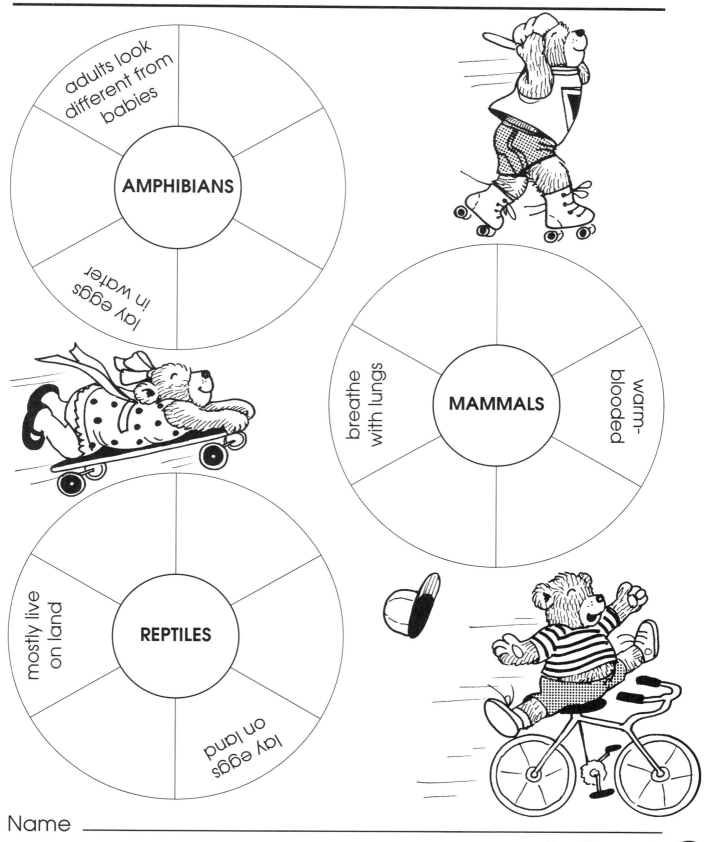

AMPHIBIANS

adults look different from babies

lay eggs in water

MAMMALS

breathe with lungs

warm-blooded

REPTILES

mostly live on land

lay eggs on land

Name _____

Use with page 18.

Vertebrate Classification

Mix-up at the Zoo

Help! Some of the zoo animals got into the wrong homes.

Find the animal in each home that does not belong.
Draw an arrow from the animal to its correct home.

Vertebrate Classification

Name _____

Basic Skills/Science 2-3

How Those Animals Behave!

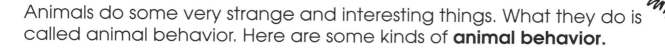

Animals do some very strange and interesting things. What they do is called animal behavior. Here are some kinds of **animal behavior.**

C Animals **camouflage** themselves for protection. This means they blend in with things around them.

A Animals **adapt** to their environment. This means they develop body parts or behaviors that help them survive.

D Animals **defend** themselves when they are in danger.

H Animals **hibernate**, or sleep, for long periods of time to save energy.

M Animals **migrate**, or move, to other places for food or breeding.

Put the correct letter by each picture to tell what kind of behavior it shows.

1. _____

2. _____

3. _____

4. _____

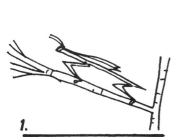

5. _____

6. _____

7. _____

8. _____

Name _____

Home, Sweet Home

This is home to one of these animals. But what is it? And which animal lives in this home? Follow the dots from 1 to 26 to find out what the home is. Color the home. Then circle the correct animal for the home. Color all the animals.

Basic Skills/Science 2-3

Who's Who in the Community?

You know that people live in communities. So do plants and animals.

What is a **community?** It is a group of consumers and producers living together in an area.

A **producer** is a living thing that makes its own food.

A **consumer** is a living thing that cannot make its own food and must eat other living things.

Find the producers. Color them **green.**

Find the consumers. Color them **other colors.**

Circle any predators (animals that eat other animals) that you see.

Name _____

Looking for Habitats

A **habitat** is a place where a living thing gets everything it needs — food, shelter, living space, the right temperature, and protection.

These plants and animals have wandered *away* from their habitats. Help them get back where they belong.

Look at the habitats on the next page (page 25). Draw each of the plants and animals below in the habitat where it belongs.

Name _____

Use with page 25.

Habitats

Basic Skills/Science 2-3

Looking for Habitats, continued . . .

A **desert** has very little moisture.

On a **grassland,** most of the plants are grass.

A **coniferous forest** has trees with needles.

A **rain forest** is very hot and wet.

Ponds, lakes, swamps, and rivers are **fresh water** habitats.

An **ocean** is a **salt water** habitat.

Name _____

Use with page 24.

Eco-Puzzle

Ecology is the study of the way plants and animals live together within their environment.

This puzzle is missing some ecology words. Write each of these words in the blank puzzle piece that is joined to the meaning of the word.

consumers	predator	food chain
scavenger	community	prey
decomposer	producers	

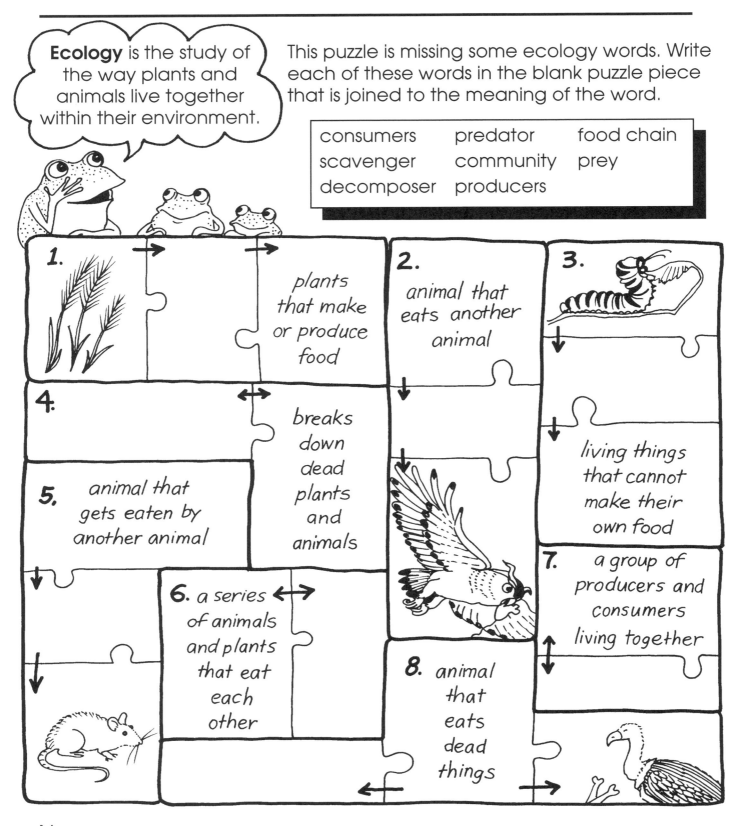

1.

plants that make or produce food

2. animal that eats another animal

3.

4.

breaks down dead plants and animals

5. animal that gets eaten by another animal

living things that cannot make their own food

6. a series of animals and plants that eat each other

7. a group of producers and consumers living together

8. animal that eats dead things

Name _____

Earth Care

The trash can is full of words that tell about pollution or ways to care for the Earth. The sentences tell some things you need to know about how pollution can harm the Earth or how you can help keep the Earth clean.

One word in each sentence is scrambled. Unscramble it. (Use the words in the trash can for correct spelling.)

1. (noPilltu) _____ is a harmful thing that can damage the environment.

2. Be careful not to (etsaw) _____ water, paper, or other supplies.

3. If you (cryceel) _____ newspaper, it can be used again.

4. Do not (rettil) _____ . Put waste in the (shrat) _____ can.

5. Sounds that harm the environment are called (osine) _____ .

6. Big ships sometimes spill (ilo) _____ in the ocean.

7. Toxic wastes are (noispo) _____ to the environment.

8. Cars, trucks, and machines put out (shaxute) _____ into the (ira) _____

9. (diAc) _____ rain contains chemicals from burning fuels.

recycle
litter
exhaust
poison
pollution
acid
noise
trash
air
waste
oil

Name _____

Pollution & Conservation

Too Much Pollution

Polly is surprised to see so much pollution.

Help her find all the different kinds of pollution shown in this picture. Put a large **X** on each example of pollution you see. How many did you find?

Name _____

Basic Skills/Science 2-3

Plenty of Bones

You are loaded with bones! If you didn't have them, your body would be all floppy like jelly. Bones are stiff. They support and hold all the softer body parts in place. It's a good thing bones are strong, because they protect important organs like the heart, lungs, brain, liver, and kidneys. Draw a line from each bone to the correct term in the box below.

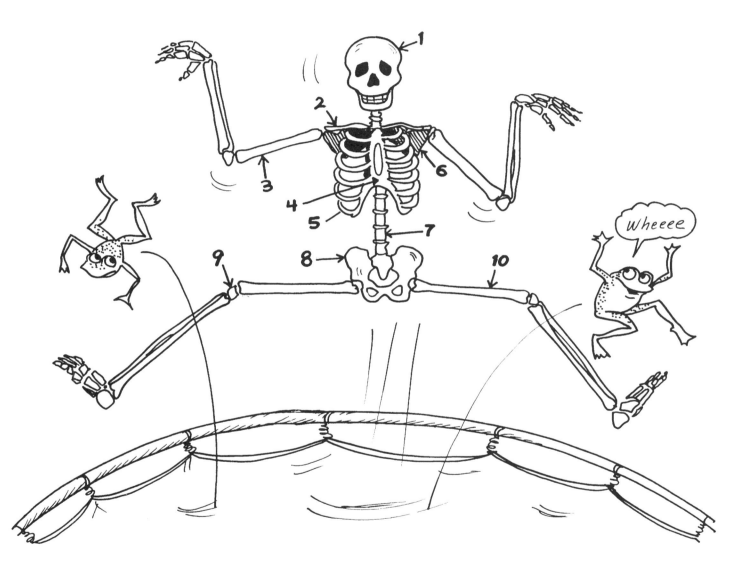

skull	collarbone	shoulder blade	humerus	kneecap
ribs	pelvis	backbone	breastbone	femur

Name _____

Skeletal System

Body Parts in Hiding

Each word in the puzzle belongs to one of these body systems.
Color the puzzle pieces these colors:

Circulatory System—blue   **Respiratory System**—green
Skeleton-Muscle System—yellow   **Nervous System**—purple
Digestive System—red   **Senses**—black

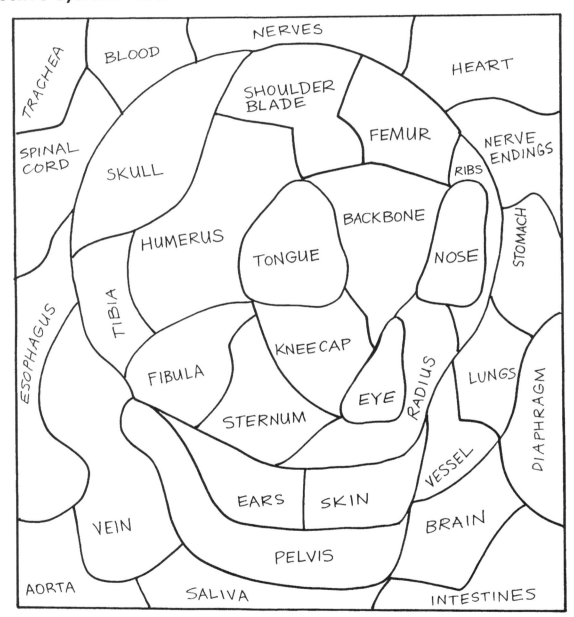

Which body part does the picture show? _____

Name _____

Body Systems

Basic Skills/Science 2-3

Body Talk

There are special words to use when you talk about the human body.
Some of these words are pictured here.

Write the body word in the space with the same number as the
matching picture.

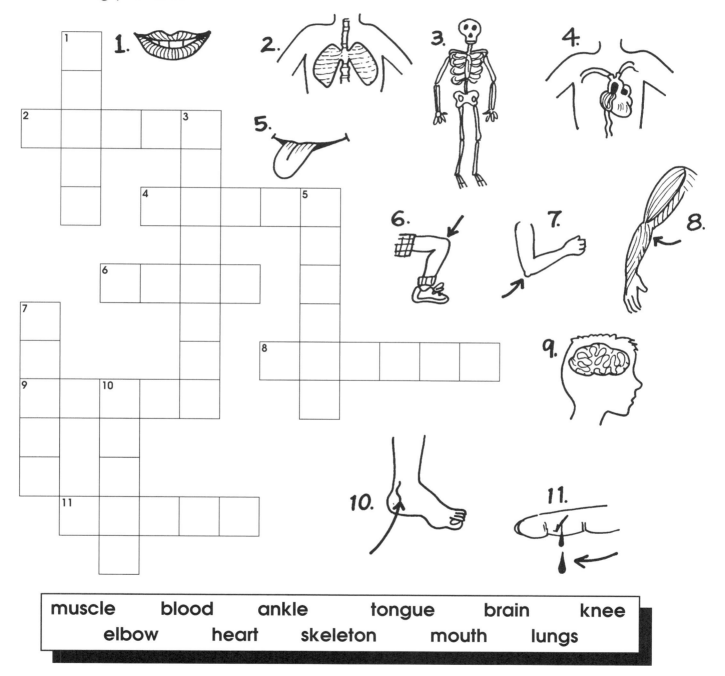

muscle	blood	ankle	tongue	brain	knee
elbow	heart	skeleton	mouth	lungs	

Name _____

Aches & Pains

Chester is a mess! He has all kinds of aches and pains. Read each complaint he has. Decide which word matches his complaint. Write the number of the complaint beside the word.

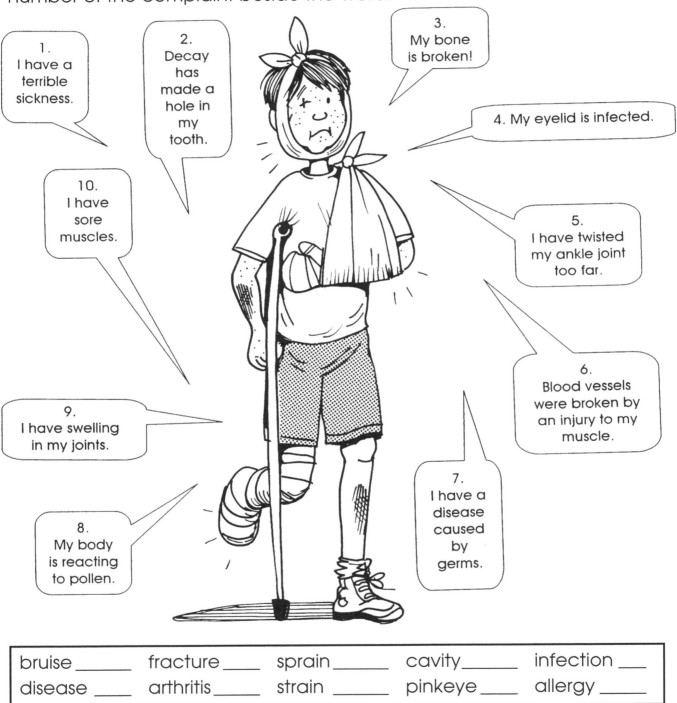

1. I have a terrible sickness.

2. Decay has made a hole in my tooth.

3. My bone is broken!

4. My eyelid is infected.

5. I have twisted my ankle joint too far.

6. Blood vessels were broken by an injury to my muscle.

7. I have a disease caused by germs.

8. My body is reacting to pollen.

9. I have swelling in my joints.

10. I have sore muscles.

bruise _____	fracture ____	sprain _____	cavity _____	infection ___
disease ____	arthritis ____	strain _____	pinkeye ____	allergy _____

Name _____

Health Opposites

There are 6 pairs of opposites shown here. In each pair, one twin is practicing a healthy behavior. The other twin is practicing something unhealthy or unsafe. Match the pairs of opposites by connecting them with a line.

Name _____

Health Behaviors

Refrigerator Inspection

Sam's refrigerator is crammed with all kinds of foods. Some of them will help him have a healthy diet.

Color the foods that are healthy for Sam to eat. Do not color foods that he should eat only in small amounts.

Name _____

Unsafe!

Several things in this picture are not safe. Find them quickly, before anybody gets hurt! Circle any unsafe situations or actions you see.

Name _____

Bodies in Space

There are things out in space called bodies. They don't look anything like our bodies. But they are out there, and many of them are moving.

Sue and Sam think they know a lot about the bodies in our solar system.

They have written down some things they think they know. Are they right?

Put **T** next to the correct statements.
Put **F** next to the ones that are not right.

_____ 1. The sun is a star.

_____ 2. The Earth turns every day.

_____ 3. The sun travels around the Earth.

_____ 4. The Earth travels around the sun.

_____ 5. The Earth travels around the moon.

_____ 6. The sun is the only star we can see.

_____ 7. The Earth is the closest planet to the sun.

_____ 8. The Earth is the largest planet in its solar system.

Name _____

Space Maze

5 astronauts are on trips through space. Color each path with the color given below to help them get to the right place.

Blue — Bob is on his way to the planet we live on.
Red — Bill is headed for the body that revolves around the Earth.
Green — Bo needs to get to the largest planet in the solar system.
Yellow — Bev is on her way to a planet that is next to Earth.
Purple — Barb wants to visit the star closest to Earth.

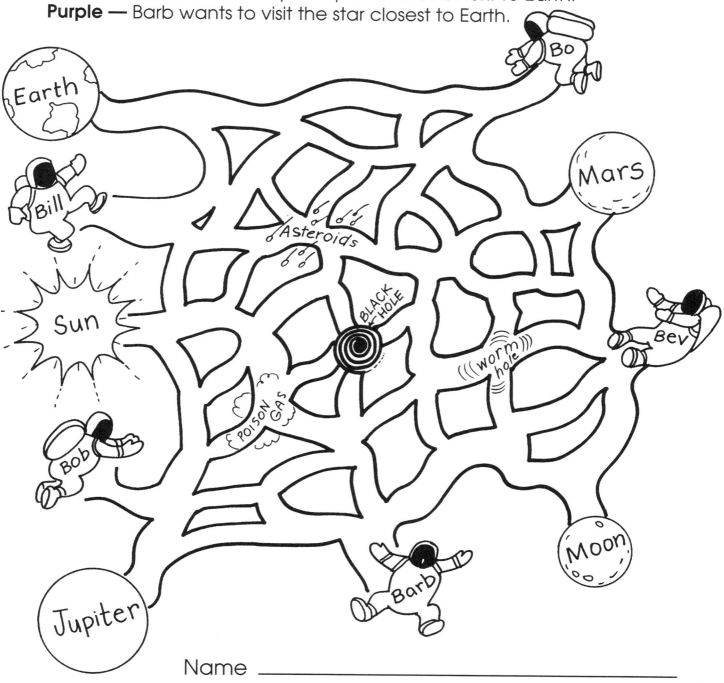

Name _____

Surface Search

The Earth's surface is covered with many different bumps, lumps, holes, and ditches. Most of these are called **landforms** or **bodies of water.**

Look at some of these landforms and bodies of water on the map on the next page (page 39). Do you know what they are? Follow the directions below to show what you know.

1. Draw a  standing on the plateau.

2. Draw two  on the iceberg.

3. Draw a flag on the mountain peak.

4. Put an on the source of the river.

5. Draw some on the hill.

6. Draw a in the ocean.

7. Draw a  in the lake.

8. Draw a  on the island.

9. Draw  on the peninsula.

10. Draw a in the waterfall.

11. Draw a going down the river.

12. Draw a in the bay.

13. Write Help! coming out of the canyon.

Name _____

Use with page 39.

Earth Surface Features

Basic Skills/Science 2-3

Surface Search, continued . . .

Name _____

Use with page 38.

Cracks & Rumbles

The Earth may look pretty solid on the surface, but lots of moving and rumbling takes place on the inside. Some of these changes inside the Earth cause big changes on the surface.

Solve this puzzle about some changes that start inside the Earth.

1. sudden movement of Earth's rock

2. melted rock that pours out of a volcano

3. dustlike matter that shoots out of a volcano

4. During an earthquake, the Earth _____ .

5. a crack in Earth's surface

6. an earthquake vibration

7. A fault is a _____ in the Earth.

8. A volcano explodes, or _____ .

9. a mountain formed by material that has been forced out of the inside of the Earth

10. the top layer of Earth

crack	tremor	lava
shakes	volcano	crust
ash	erupts	fault
	earthquake	

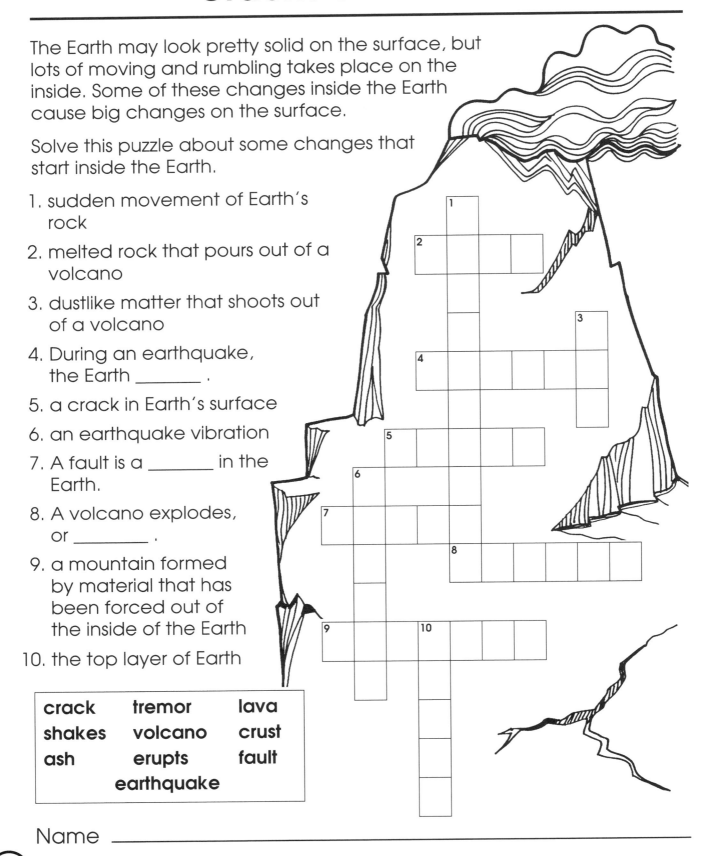

Name _____

Slow? Or Sudden?

The Earth is always changing. Sometimes it happens very slowly. Sometimes it happens fast—all of a sudden! It is wearing away and moving.

Clyde has gotten himself in the middle of many Earth changes. What is happening around Clyde? Draw a line from each picture to a word in the box that describes the change. Then tell whether the change is fast or slow by circling the right word.

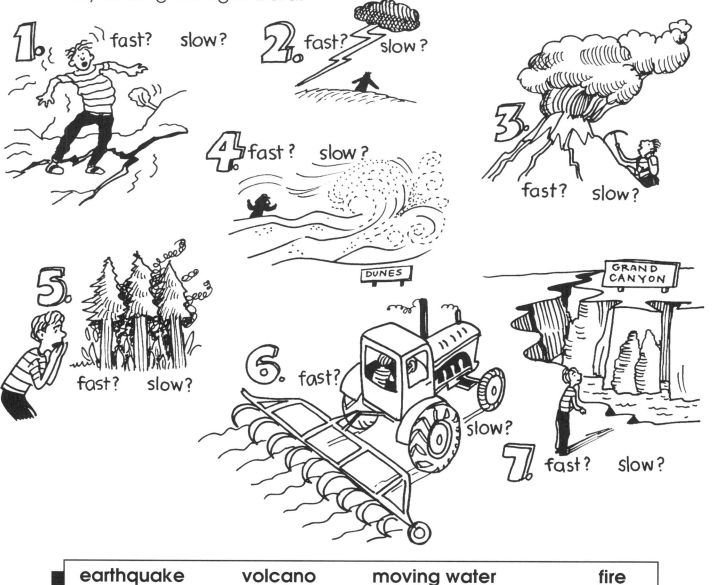

| earthquake | volcano | moving water | fire |
| lightning | wind | people & machines | |

Name _____

Underwater Treasure Hunt

Help Dianna, the diver, find her way through the ocean to the treasure. Use a crayon to follow the path of words that name things found in the ocean. Don't let her wander into any wrong corners of the ocean bottom.

salt water   fresh water   pine cones

lake   waves   tulips   lizard

tundra   shells   jellyfish

apples   oil   rocket   globe   pen   starfish

wind   currents   shipwrecks   kelp   sand   crabs

alligator   sharks   blizzard   lightning bug   pond   cactus   cocoon

whales   creek

Name _____

Deep-Sea Facts

Where is the surfer? Where is the diver? Where is the lobster? If you know some facts about the ocean, you can answer these questions! Use the picture to find the answers. Write the answer to each question.

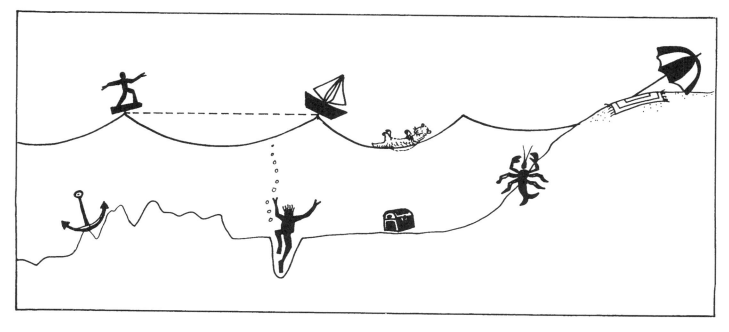

1. What are on the crests of the waves? _____ and _____

2. What is in the wave trough?_____

3. What is on the beach?_____

4. The wavelength is the distance
   between the surfer and the _____ .

5. What is on the ocean plain? _____

6. What is on the continental shelf? _____

7. What is on the underwater mountain range?_____

8. What is in the ocean trench?_____

Name _____

What's the Matter?

Matter is anything that takes up space and has weight.
There are 3 kinds of matter: solid, liquid, and gas.

Find 5 squares that have to do with solids. Color them red.
Find 6 squares that have to with liquid. Color them blue.
Find 5 squares that have to do with gases.
Color them yellow.

solid		has a definite shape	
has a definite size			**liquid**
has no definite shape		has no definite shape	has no definite size
gas	can be poured		has a definite size

Name _____

A Matter of Change

Things are changing! Jonah's ice cubes disappeared when he left his lemonade in the sun. His wet hair dried, too! Matter comes in three forms (or states): solid, liquid, and gas. Each of these can change to other states. These changes have names.

For each name, tell what change is happening.

1.   **MELT** = a change from _____ to _____

2.   **FREEZE** = a change from _____ to _____

3.   **EVAPORATE** = a change from _____ to _____

4.   **CONDENSE** = a change from _____ to _____

Tell which kind of change is happening in each picture. Write one of the words above.

5. _____

6. _____

7. _____

8. _____

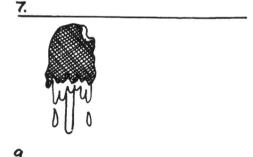

9. _____

10. _____

Name _____

The Air up There

The kites describe some things about the air around the Earth. Who is flying these kites? Draw a string from each kite to the word that matches it. Use a different color of string for each kite.

Name _____

Air • Atmosphere

Basic Skills/Science 2-3

Ready for Anything

Tara is going on vacation. She doesn't know what kind of weather to expect, so she's decided to be ready for anything!

Read each weather report she might hear. Find the word that names that kind of weather condition. Write the word under the report.

1. "Watch out for a powerful, whirling funnel of air."

2. "There will be no clouds today."

3. "Droplets of water in the clouds will join together and pour down."

4. "Temperatures will rise to uncomfortable levels today."

blizzard   dry   hot
lightning
sunny
tornado
rain   windy

5. "The air will move at very fast speeds tonight."

6. "Be prepared for heavy snow along with high winds."

7. "Be ready for a storm with flashes of electricity."

8. "There will be no precipitation this week."

Name _____

Lost in the Clouds

This traveling bird is lost in the clouds. But what kind of cloud is he on?

A **cloud** forms when air cools. The cooling air causes water vapor (a gas) to condense into tiny drops of water. Sometimes these drops freeze. These tiny drops of water are clouds.

This page describes different kinds of clouds. Read about them.
Then look at the pictures on the next page.
Write the name of the cloud where each bird is flying or resting.

cumulus—large, thick, puffy clouds with a flat bottom
Cumulus clouds usually come with good weather.

cirrus—thin, wispy, white clouds that are high above the ground
They tell us the weather will change.

stratus—low, gray blanket of clouds that covers the sky
Stratus clouds often produce rain.

cumulonimbus—tall, towering clouds
They often produce rain, snow, or hail.

fog—stratus clouds that are very close to the ground

Name _____

Use with page 49.

Clouds & Weather

Lost in the Clouds, continued . . .

Color the pictures on both pages.

Name _____

Use with page 48.

Weather & Clouds

Pushing & Pulling

What's missing in this picture?

Draw what's missing in the picture.
What would make these things move?

A **force** is a push or
pull on something.

Name _____

Hidden Machines

There are 6 kinds of simple machines. Find 1 or more of each of these in the picture. Color it or outline it in color.

Machines do work.

A **machine** is used to change the amount or direction of a force.

lever
screw

inclined plane
wheel & axle

wedge
pulley

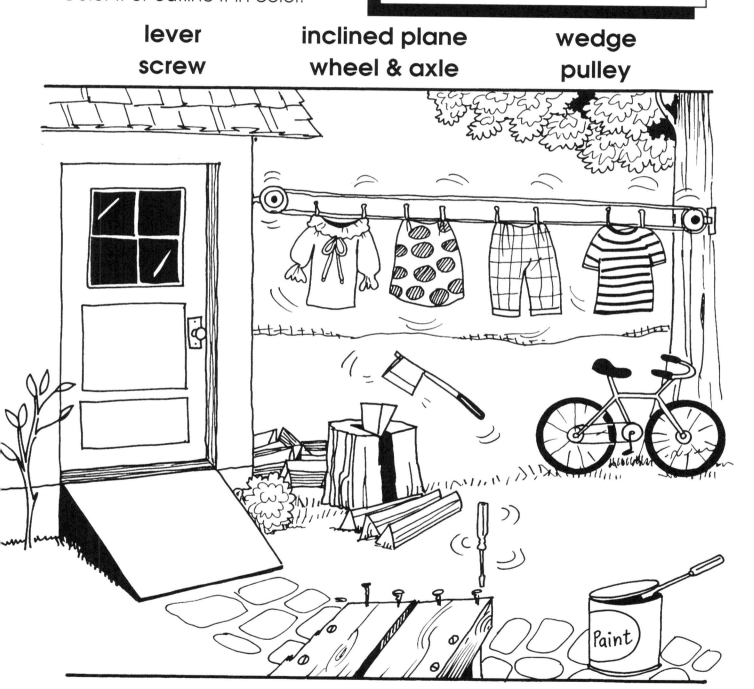

Name _____

The Sound of the Drum

When Todd hits his drum, a sound is made.
The sound travels through the air to his ears.

Each drum has a word about sound.
Each pair of drumsticks has a description to match one word.
Find the sticks to match each drum. Draw a line to connect them.

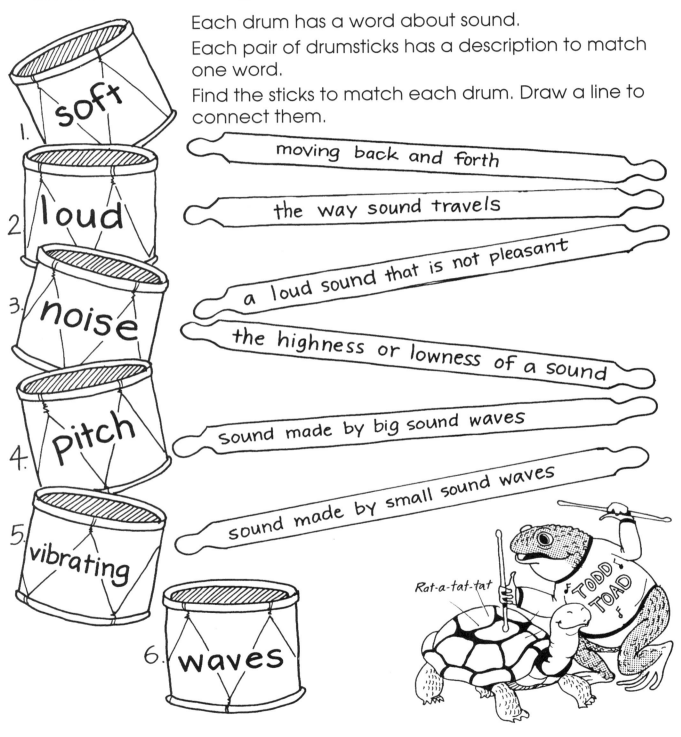

1. soft

2. loud

3. noise

4. pitch

5. vibrating

6. waves

moving back and forth

the way sound travels

a loud sound that is not pleasant

the highness or lowness of a sound

sound made by big sound waves

sound made by small sound waves

Rat-a-tat-tat

TODD TOAD

Name _____

Hot Words

Hiding in this puzzle are some words that have something to do with heat. Read the clues. Then find the word. The clues tell you what color to color each puzzle piece. Look out for hot words!

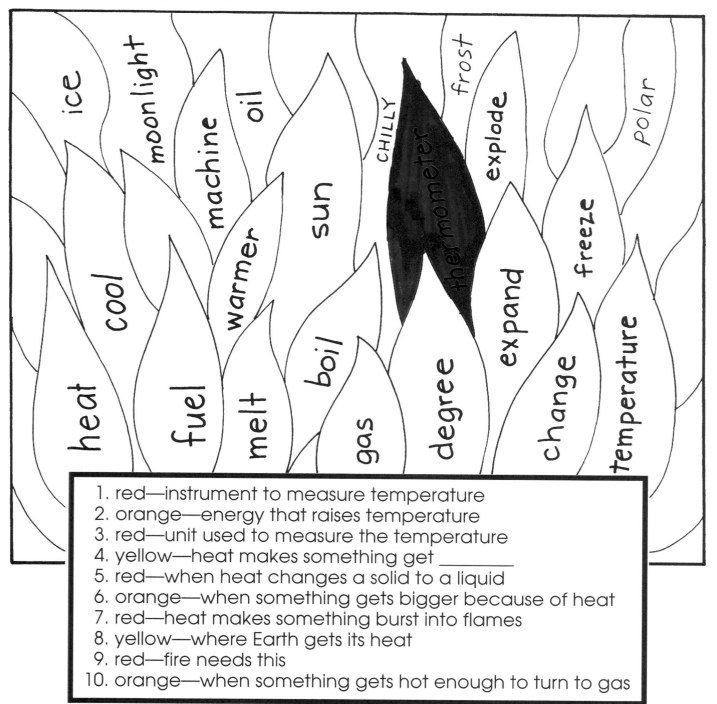

ice
moonlight
machine
oil
frost
explode
polar
CHILLY
thermometer
freeze
sun
warmer
cool
expand
temperature
heat
fuel
melt
boil
gas
degree
change

1. red—instrument to measure temperature
2. orange—energy that raises temperature
3. red—unit used to measure the temperature
4. yellow—heat makes something get _____
5. red—when heat changes a solid to a liquid
6. orange—when something gets bigger because of heat
7. red—heat makes something burst into flames
8. yellow—where Earth gets its heat
9. red—fire needs this
10. orange—when something gets hot enough to turn to gas

Name _____

Where Would You Find It?

Would you find a **patella** in your fruit salad?

Would you find a **vitamin** in the solar system?

Would you find a **pulley** in your blood?

Look at each science word. Tell where you would find it. Circle the correct answer.

Where would you find ....

1. a patella?
   a. in your skeleton
   b. in a fruit salad
   c. inside a plant leaf

2. a planet?
   a. going around the Earth
   b. going around the sun
   c. floating in your blood

3. a stomata?
   a. on a plant's leaf
   b. in your stomach
   c. on a glacier

4. a cloud?
   a. on an amphibian
   b. in the atmosphere
   c. in a sound wave

5. a predator?
   a. in a plant seed
   b. circling Mars
   c. eating an animal

6. a casting?
   a. in a worm's burrow
   b. in your ear
   c. in a storm cloud

7. an inclined plane?
   a. in a flower
   b. in your digestive system
   c. in a machine

8. a conifer?
   a. orbiting the sun
   b. growing in a forest
   c. hibernating underground

Name _____

Science Words to Know

adaptation—a way an animal changes to survive in its environment

allergy—a reaction of the body to something, such as pollen

air—layer of gases around the Earth

amphibian—a cold-blooded animal with a backbone that can live both on land and in water

arachnid—an 8-legged animal with no antennae

atmosphere—the air around the Earth

behavior—any response an animal makes to its environment

bird—a warm-blooded animal with a backbone, feathers, and a beak

bristles—short, stiff hair that helps worms move

bruise—blood vessels broken by an injury to a muscle

burrows—underground tunnels that are homes to some animals

camouflage—a way that an animal blends into its environment

castings—lumps of dirt that have passed through an earthworm's body

clouds—groups of tiny drops of ice or water that hang together in the air

community—a group of plants and animals that live together in an area

condense—to change from a gas to a liquid

consumer—an animal that eats plants or animals to live

continental shelf—the slope of land underneath the water of the ocean

crest—the highest point on a wave

crust—the outer layer of the Earth

disease—a sickness

earthquake—a sudden movement of the rocks in the Earth's surface

energy—being able to work

environment—everything around you

evaporate—to change from a liquid to a gas

Copyright ©1998 by Incentive Publications, Inc., Nashville, TN.
Basic Skills/Science 2-3

fault—a crack in the Earth's surface

fish—a cold-blooded animal with a backbone that lives in water, breathes with gills, and is covered with scales

force—the push or pull that moves an object

fossil—a print or part of an animal that lived long ago

freeze—to change from a liquid to a solid by becoming colder

fracture—a break in a bone

fuel—something that is burned to make heat

gas—a form of matter that has no definite size or shape

germination—the beginning growth of a seed into a plant

glacier—a large body of ice that moves

habitat—the place where an animal or plant lives

hibernate—to sleep for a long period of time to save energy

insect—an animal with 3 body segments, 6 legs, and 2 antennae

invertebrate—an animal that has no backbone

kelp—brown seaweed

landform—shapes of land on the surface of the Earth

lava—melted rock that flows out of a volcano

liquid—a form of matter that has a definite size but no definite shape

litter—trash scattered around the environment

mammal—a warm-blooded animal with a backbone that is covered with fur or hair

melt—to change from a solid to a liquid by becoming warmer

migrate—to move to another place for food or breeding

noise—a sound that is not pleasant

nutrition—the foods needed for a living thing to survive

orbit—the path a planet follows around the sun

peninsula—a narrow piece of land with water on all sides but one

petal—the outer, protective part of a flower

photosynthesis—the process in which plants use sunlight to make food

pistil—the part of a flower that contains the ovary where fruit grows

pitch—the highness or lowness of a sound

plain—the bottom of the ocean

planet—a body in space that orbits around the sun

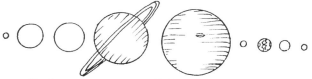

pollutant—something that is harmful to the environment

predator—an animal that eats other animals

prey—an animal that is eaten by another animal

producer—living thing that makes its own food

recycle—to use things again so they are not wasted

reptile—a cold-blooded animal with a backbone and dry, scaly skin

sepal—the outside part of the flower that protects the bud

skeleton—the bones inside a living thing

skin—the outer covering of the body

solar system—the sun and the planets that revolve around it

scavenger—an animal that eats dead things

solid—a form of matter that has a definite size and shape

sprain—a joint that is twisted too far

stamen—the part of the flower that produces pollen

strain—sore muscles

stomata—tiny openings in a leaf that allow air to get in

temperature—a measurement of how warm something is

trench—the deepest part of the ocean floor

trough—the space between the crests of waves

vertebrate—an animal that has a backbone

vibrate—to move back and forth

volcano—a mountain formed by melted rock that comes from the inside of the Earth

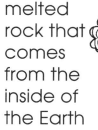

weather—the conditions of the air outside

wind—moving air

work—happens whenever an object is moved

Science Skills Test

Write the letter of the word that matches each definition.

1. _____ process where plants use sunlight to make food
2. _____ plant part that holds plants in the ground
3. _____ parts of the flower that produce pollen
4. _____ part of the flower that makes seeds
5. _____ tiny openings in leaves that take in air

a. flower
b. stomata
c. roots
d. stamens
e. photosynthesis

Write the letter of the word that matches each definition.

6. _f_ animal with a backbone
7. _h_ animal with 8 legs and no antennae
8. _i_ animal with 6 legs and 2 antennae
9. _g_ animal with no backbone
10. _j_ animal with many segments and bristles

f. vertebrate
g. invertebrate
h. arachnid
i. insect
j. earthworm

Circle the correct answer or answers.

11. Which plant part makes food?

12. Which things are part of the circulatory system?

13. Which thing is NOT alive?

14. Which animal belongs in a grassland habitat?

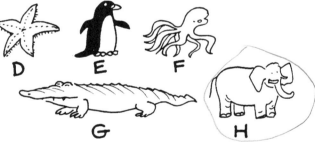

15. Which picture shows germination?

Write the letter of the word that matches each definition.

16. _b_ has gills and scales
17. _d_ covered with feathers
18. _e_ covered with dry scales
19. _a_ covered with fur or hair
20. _c_ can breathe on land or in water

a. mammals
b. birds
c. amphibians
d. fish
e. reptiles

Name _____

Science Skills Test

Circle the correct answer or answers.

21. Which of these living things are producers?

22. Which of these are consumers?

23. Which one of these is a predator?

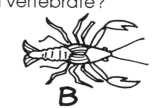

24. Which flower part is a petal?

25. Which animal is a vertebrate?

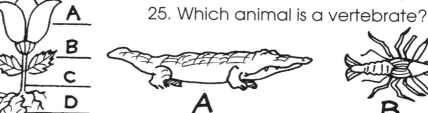

Write the letter of the word that matches each definition.

26. _____ sleep to save energy

27. _____ fight back to protect itself

28. _____ move somewhere else for a while

29. _____ change to survive in the environment

30. _____ blend into the environment

a. camouflage

b. hibernate

c. migrate

d. defend

e. adapt

Circle the correct answer or answers.

31. Which animal is an insect?

34. Which animal is NOT a reptile?

32. Which animal is an arachnid?

35. Which animal is NOT a mammal?

33. Which end of this earthworm is the tail?

A   B

Name _____

Science Skills Test

Write the letter of the word that matches each definition.

36. _____ break in a bone

37. _____ a muscle or joint stretched too far

38. _____ a body's reaction to something like pollen

39. _____ an illness

40. _____ hole caused by decay in a tooth

a. fracture

b. cavity

c. allergy

d. disease

e. sprain

Circle the correct answer or answers.

41. Which animals are cold-blooded?

A   B   C

42. Which animals are warm-blooded?

D   E   F   G

43. Which animal can live both on land and in water?

A   B   C   D

44. Which picture shows an animal hibernating?

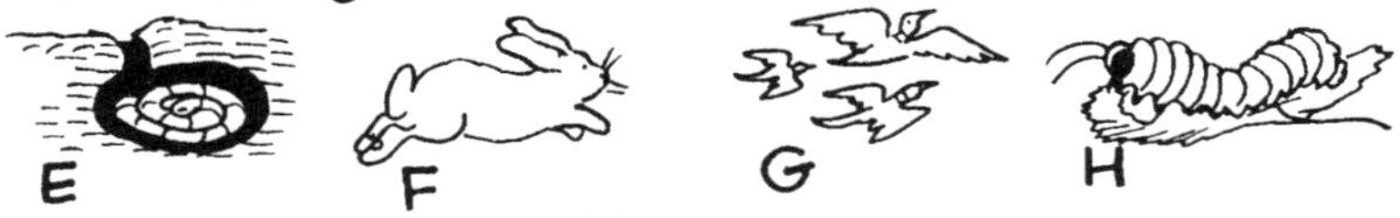

E   F   G   H

45. Which bone is the ribs?

A   B   C   D

Write the letter of the word that matches each definition.

46. ____ a crack in the Earth's surface

47. ____ a large mass of ice that moves

48. ____ when a volcano explodes

49. ____ the layer of air around the Earth

50. ____ melted rock that flows from a crack in the Earth

a. atmosphere

b. fault

c. eruption

d. lava

e. glacier

Circle the correct answer or answers.

51. Which one travels around the sun?

A   B   C

52. Which is a peninsula?

D   E   F

Name _____

53. Which shows the molecules in a gas?

54. Which swimmer is on the crest of the wave?

55. Which does this picture show?
   A. freezing
   B. evaporation   C. melting

56. An animal that eats dead animals is
   A. prey
   B. a producer   C. a scavenger

57. An animal that eats another animal is called the
   D. predator
   E. decomposer   F. producer

58. The radius, ulna, and humerus are bones in the
   A. arm   B. leg   C. back

59. The tibia, fibula, and femur are bones in the
   D. ankle   E. arm   F. leg

60. Which one of these is caused by germs?
   A. a bruise
   B. an infection   C. a fracture

61. Which cloud is a cumulonimbus?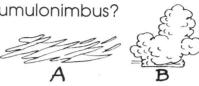

62. Which machine is an inclined plane?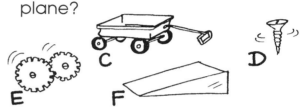

63. Which machine is a pulley?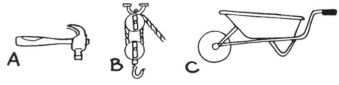

64. Which one of these is an island?

65. Which boat is at the mouth of the river?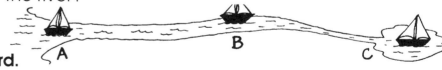

Write the letter of the matching word.

66. ____ a push or a pull   a. vibrate
67. ____ to move back and forth   b. pitch
68. ____ the way sound travels   c. melt
69. ____ a change from a solid to a liquid   d. waves
70. ____ the highness or lowness of a sound e. force

Name _____

Answer Key

Skills Test

1. e	19. a	36. a	53. A
2. c	20. c	37. e	54. D
3. d	21. A & C	38. c	55. C
4. a		39. d	56. C
5. b	22. E & G	40. b	57. D
6. f		41. A & B	58. A
7. h	23. B		59. F
8. i	24. A	42. D, E, & F	60. B
9. g	25. A		61. B
10. j	26. b	43. C	62. F
11. B	27. d	44. E	63. B
12. E & G	28. c	45. D	64. D
	29. e	46. b	65. A
13. A	30. a	47. e	66. e
14. H	31. A	48. c	67. a
15. A	32. F	49. a	68. d
16. d	33. A	50. d	69. c
17. b	34. D	51. B	70. b
18. e	35. A	52. D	

Skills Exercises

page 10

Check to see that students have completed drawings to adequately picture the life characteristics.

page 11

1. roots   3. leaves   5. cone
2. stem   4. flower

Check to see that students have added roots, leaves, and flower to the plant and trunk, roots, and cones to the tree.

page 12

Check to see that students have adequately depicted the stages of the cycle.

page 13

Across 1. carbon   2. sunlight   3. stomata
4. oxygen   5. leaves
Down 1. chlorophyll

page 14

1. B   3. H   5. D   7. G
2. F   4. E   6. C   8. A

page 15

Animals with backbones: rabbit, ostrich, squirrel, bird, snake, crocodile, bear, elephant, frog, turtle, pig, shark, person

page 16

Red Circle—insects: 1, 3, 4, 6, 8, 11
Blue Box—arachnids: 2, 5, 9, 12

page 17

1. segments   4. darker   7. muscles
2. burrow   5. pointed
3. bristles   6. castings

pages 18-19

BIRDS
- feathers
- warm-blooded
- most fly
- wings

FISH
- fins
- breathe only with gills
- scales
- shark picture

AMPHIBIANS
- live on land or water
- cold-blooded
- smooth, moist skin
- frog picture

MAMMALS
- monkey picture
- hair or fur
- give milk to young
- babies grow inside mothers

REPTILES
- cold-blooded
- scaly, dry skin
- alligator picture
- snake picture

page 20

Bird Cage: snake—Reptiles
Fish Tank: cat—Mammal House
Mammal House: alligator—Reptiles
Reptiles: bird—Bird Cage
Amphibians: rabbit—Mammal House

page 21

1. C   3. A   5. D   7. D
2. C   4. D   6. H   8. M

page 22

The home is a cactus.
The animal is a lizard.

page 23

The producers are all plants.
The consumers are all animals.
Predators are owl and fox.

pages 24-25

Students should add the following:

To desert—cactus, lizard, rattlesnake, camel

To grassland—lion, elephant

To coniferous forest—pine tree, owl, moose, wolf

To rain forest—monkey, parrot, tree

To pond—beaver, turtle, frog, fish

To ocean—whale, starfish, fish, crab, coral

page 26

1. producers
2. predator
3. consumers
4. decomposer
5. prey
6. food chain
7. community
8. scavenger

page 27

1. Pollution
2. waste
3. recycle
4. litter, trash
5. noise
6. oil
7. poison
8. exhaust, air
9. Acid

page 28

Examples of pollution pictured are:
- airplane exhaust
- factory fumes
- car, truck, and boat fumes
- pollution into water from factory
- tractor spraying
- airplane noise

page 29

1. skull
2. collarbone
3. humerus
4. breastbone
5. ribs
6. shoulderblade
7. backbone
8. pelvis
9. kneecap
10. femur

page 30

Circulatory—blood, vein, aorta, heart, vessel

Skeleton-Muscle—ribs, backbone, shoulder blade, humerus, tibia, sternum, kneecap, pelvis, femur, skull, fibula, radius

Digestive—intestines, esophagus, saliva, stomach

Respiratory—lungs, trachea, diaphragm

Nervous—brain, nerves, spinal cord, nerve endings

Senses—eyes, tongue, nose, ears, skin

The body part is a skull.

page 31

1. mouth
2. lungs
3. skeleton
4. heart
5. tongue
6. knee
7. elbow
8. muscle
9. brain
10. ankle
11. blood

page 32

1. disease
2. cavity
3. fracture
4. pinkeye
5. sprain
6. bruise
7. infection
8. allergy
9. arthritis
10. strain

page 33

Matching pictures

1—E
2—A
3—F
4—B
5—D
6—C

page 34

Answers may vary. Discuss possibilities with students.

Healthy foods:
- peas
- carrots
- vegetarian pizza
- spaghetti sauce
- orange juice
- fruit
- milk
- carrot juice
- eggs
- yogurt
- bananas
- vegetables
- turkey
- tomatoes

page 35

Answers may vary. Discuss possibilities with students.

Unsafe situations:
- broken window
- broken ladder
- paint
- dog
- matches
- bicycle
- car
- electrical wires
- ball going into street
- lightning

page 36

1. T
2. T
3. F
4. T
5. F
6. F
7. F
8. F

page 37

Bob — Blue path—to Earth

Bill — Red path—to moon

Bo — green path—to Jupiter

Bev — yellow path—to Mars

Barb — purple path—to sun

pages 38-39

Check to see that pictures are drawn in appropriate places.

page 40

1. earthquake
2. lava
3. ash
4. shakes
5. fault
6. tremor
7. crack
8. erupts
9. volcano
10. crust

page 41

Answers may vary somewhat.

1. earthquake—fast
2. lightning—fast
3. volcano—fast
4. wind—fast (or slow)
5. fire—fast
6. people & machines—fast
7. moving water—slow

page 42

ocean words to follow:
salt water—waves—shells—jellyfish—
starfish—crabs—sand—kelp—
shipwrecks—currents—sharks—whales

page 43

1. surfer, sailboat
2. otter
3. umbrella
4. sailboat
5. treasure chest
6. lobster
7. anchor
8. diver

page 44

solid—definite shape—close together
molecules—picture of ring—definite
size—"solid"
liquid—definite size—molecules farther
apart—picture of rain—no definite
shape—can be poured—"liquid"
gas—picture of balloon—molecules
farthest apart—no definite shape—
no definite size—"gas"

page 45

1. solid to liquid
2. liquid to solid
3. liquid to gas
4. gas to liquid
5. evaporate
6. freeze
7. condense (or evaporate) depends on
   explanation of what is happening
8. melt
9. melt
10. condense

page 46

1. air
2. atmosphere
3. evaporate
4. condense
5. water
6. oceans

page 47

1. tornado
2. sunny
3. rain
4. hot
5. windy
6. blizzard
7. lightning
8. dry

pages 48-49

1. cumulonimbus
2. cirrus
3. stratus
4. cumulus
5. fog

page 50

Some missing forces:
wind—tree, kite, water, sailboat, leaves
people—rake, jump rope, wagon, pogo
stick, ball, swing, ping pong
dog or other animal—girl

page 51

lever— screwdriver opening paint
can
inclined plane— ramp to house
screws— screws in wood, door
knob
wedge— axe and wedge in wood
wheel & axle— bike
pulley— clothesline

page 52

1. sound made by small sound waves
2. sound made by big sound waves
3. a loud sound that is not pleasant
4. the highness or lowness of a sound
5. moving back and forth
6. the way sound travels

page 53

1. thermometer
2. heat
3. degree
4. warmer
5. melt
6. expand
7. explode
8. sun
9. fuel
10. boil

page 54

1. a
2. b
3. a
4. b
5. c
6. a
7. c
8. b